Turning the Tide for TURTLES

Linda Purcell as told to Lisa Rao

Contents

Rigby®

A Harcourt Achieve Imprint

www.Rigby.com
1-800-531-5015

Chapter One

A Love of the Sea and Its Creatures

The sea has always been a magical place for me, ever since I was a little girl.

My name is Linda Purcell, and I grew up on the southern coast of Connecticut in a small town called East Norwalk. When I was a child, the beach was within walking distance of my home, so I spent a lot of time there. This beach was not actually on the ocean, but on the Long Island Sound, which is a large body of water that runs into the ocean. That didn't make any difference to me. I loved the water! I went to the beach all year round.

I have also always loved sea animals. The first sea creature I remember trying to rescue was a sea bird that had somehow been trapped in some ice one winter. I guess you could say I was an animal rescuer even as a child.

Whenever I would see an animal in trouble, even if the animal was on TV or in a movie, it would upset me. I knew that someday I would do all I could to help animals in danger. I just didn't know exactly when or how.

I have always loved the sea and sea animals, so I knew I wanted a job that would let me work with both.

3

Sea Turtles: Amazing Animals

If you had asked me when I was younger which sea animal I liked best, my first answer would be, "I love them all!" However, sea turtles have become the most interesting to me. Turtles have been around since before the dinosaurs were alive (about 200 million years ago). Still, there is much we don't know about them.

When sea turtles are ready to lay eggs, they find their way back to the same beach where they were hatched. How do you think they find their way?

We do know that after sea turtles hatch from eggs, they travel all over the world. Then they come back to the beach where they were born to lay their own eggs. Wondering how sea turtles find their way home made them even more interesting to me.

When I was a little girl playing along the sandy shore, I had no way of knowing that someday sea turtles would be a huge part of my life!

Sea Turtles in Trouble

All around the world, sea turtles are in trouble. It's true that they have outlived the dinosaurs. However, they're no match for modern **predators**—namely humans. Some people hunt turtles for their meat and shells.

Today the world's population of sea turtles has become dangerously small. Scientists warn that if people do nothing to protect them, loggerhead and leatherback turtles could be **extinct** within thirty years.

Turtles move very slowly, and they like to stay in places that are familiar to them. When sea turtles find a beach they like, they return to that same spot to nest over and over again. This makes it easy for turtle hunters to find them.

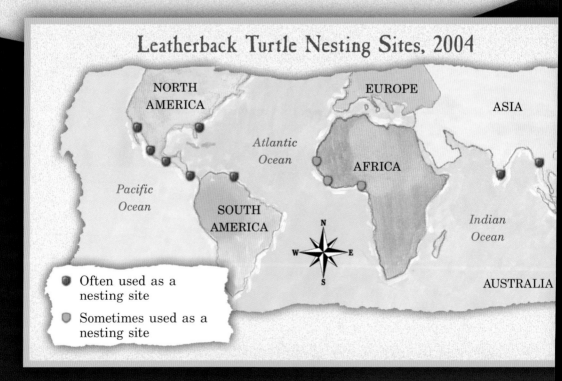

Leatherback Turtle Nesting Sites, 2004

NORTH AMERICA

EUROPE

ASIA

Atlantic Ocean

AFRICA

Pacific Ocean

SOUTH AMERICA

Indian Ocean

N
W   E
S

AUSTRALIA

🔴 Often used as a nesting site

🔵 Sometimes used as a nesting site

Sea turtles face other dangers, too. Some get caught in fishing nets, and others die from ocean **pollution**. Shrimp nets are also a big cause of sea turtle deaths. When sea turtles get caught in the large nets, they can't escape. Sea turtles can't swim backward, so they aren't able to swim out of the net. About 2,300 leatherback turtles are killed in U.S. shrimp nets each year.

Why do you think it is easy for sea turtles to get caught in fishing nets?

A Promising Program

Fortunately there are sea turtle protection programs set up around the world. These programs show that saving sea turtles is possible. In fact, at some major nesting beaches in Mexico, the turtles are making a comeback. There are currently 27 programs funded by the Mexican government to help sea turtles. These programs are designed to rescue sick and hurt sea turtles and nurse them back to health.

As part of my job, I help sea turtles of all sizes, large and small, that have become sick or hurt.

In 1990 Mexico **banned** the hunting of sea turtles. As a result, in 2005 there were four times as many sea turtle nests in Mexico as there were in 1990.

In addition to banning the hunting of sea turtles, government agents now closely watch the beaches, guarding nesting sea turtles and their eggs. The Mexican people are also learning about sea turtle protection. Scientists have hatched similar sea turtle success stories around the world.

Chapter Two

A Dream Realized

In 1996 I moved to Holden Beach, North Carolina. When I arrived there, I didn't know anyone. However, one day I found a flyer about a sea turtle rescue program. I called the phone number listed on the paper and talked to the program director. She asked if I wanted to **volunteer** as a "turtle person" in the Holden Beach Turtle Watch program. I immediately knew that I had to help protect the local sea turtles.

Nesting at Holden Beach

Holden Beach is home to both loggerhead and green turtles. There is a "turtle season," which is when sea turtles come to lay their eggs. Turtle season at Holden Beach begins at the end of May or early June each year and lasts until August or September. During this time a female sea turtle will come on shore five to seven times to lay eggs.

loggerhead turtle

green turtle

The mother sea turtle arrives at night to prepare her nest. She crawls to a place above the high-water line on the shore, past where the waves can reach. Once she has chosen a spot, she digs a hole in the sand. Her back flippers work quickly, digging a deep, narrow hole. When she feels the hole is deep enough to keep her babies safe, the mother starts laying her eggs.

When the mother has finished laying her eggs, she uses her flippers to cover her nest with sand. As she slowly makes her way back to the sea, she hides her tracks as best she can. The whole nesting process takes about two hours. The eggs hatch 55 to 65 days later, but by then the mother has swum on to other parts of the ocean and will never see her babies.

The program director told me that she expected more than 4,000 baby sea turtles to hatch that summer on Holden Beach! I couldn't wait to see all the tiny turtles for the first time!

At Holden Beach I learned that each turtle nest can contain 60 to 70 rubbery eggs that are about the size of a golf ball.

Problems for the Turtles

Sea turtles always return to their **natal beach** to lay their eggs. But imagine how these turtles feel when they return to find their favorite nesting sites replaced with cottages, vacation homes, and hotels!

Instead of giving up, the turtles search the beach for any loose soil that is above the high-water mark. If they can't find any good places to nest, they will dig along the edges of dirt roads and driveways. This is very dangerous for baby sea turtles. When a nest is far from the water, the babies must travel a long way before reaching the ocean's safety.

What might a sea turtle do if it returned to this beach in order to lay eggs?

Pollution is another big problem for nesting sea turtles. If a beach is filled with trash or broken branches from storms, a nesting turtle is in serious trouble. She may become tired while trying to find a good spot. If that happens, the turtle most likely will dig her nest too close to the sea, which means that the nest could be flooded and the babies might die.

Chapter Three

The Turtle People at Work

Whenever the other volunteers and I find a sea turtle nest on Holden Beach, we decide if we need to **relocate** it. If the nest is in an unsafe place, it has to be moved. If things look OK, we simply put a wire fence over the nest to keep animals from digging up the eggs. Then we put stakes around the nest and rope it off.

The first sign that the babies have begun to hatch is a pit that forms in the sand. This happens because the babies at the bottom of the nest usually hatch first, and as they make their way to the surface, sand falls into the nest.

Once we see the pit form, we dig a trench from the nest toward the ocean. The trench will help lead the baby sea turtles to the sea. We then rope off the trench to keep people from walking across it.

Each volunteer adopts a nest to watch. On the 50th day after the eggs have been laid, we begin to watch the nest nightly.

I helped put a nest plate, or sign, two feet in front of the nest so beach-goers know that it is against the law to disturb the nest.

DO NOT REMOVE
SEA TURTLE
NEST

The Big Night

Our motto at Holden Beach is "sea turtles dig the dark." This is because baby sea turtles, or **hatchlings**, use moonlight shining on the water to find the sea. On the night that we expect the baby turtles to hatch, the town turns off the streetlights facing the beach. Streetlights could confuse the hatchlings and make them crawl toward the street instead of into the sea, so we want to have darkness everywhere we can, except over the water.

On turtle-hatching nights, we put signs along the beach reminding people to keep their lights off. We sometimes even knock on doors and politely remind people to turn off their porchlights. On the beach, we put red or orange cloth over our flashlights to dim their glow.

The First Tiny Movement

We are all quiet. The only sound is the soft lapping of waves hitting the shore. We wait patiently for the first hatchling to make its appearance.

Finally we see the tiniest of movements! It seems as if the sand is shifting one grain at a time. A tiny head appears, followed by one flipper, then two, as the first hatchling digs its way out of the nest. Soon a line of tiny turtles wiggles across the beach.

I try to stay quiet and calm, but I can barely contain my excitement when I see tiny hatchlings dig out from their nests!

To the Sea!

The newborn sea turtles are not even two inches long, but they immediately start their journey from the nest to the sea. As the baby turtles make their way down to the water, seagulls flying overhead start diving to collect a meal. It's our job to keep the birds away and to make sure the hatchlings get to the ocean safely.

Some hatchlings wander in the wrong direction, waddling up the beach instead of toward the water. We gently turn them around but do not carry them. It is important that they find their own way since someday it will help them find their way back to this beach when it is time to lay their own eggs.

How do you think sea turtles know which way to go to reach the ocean?

There is no way of knowing how long these hatchlings will live. Females will spend 10 to 20 years at sea before they return to nest. Male turtles never return to land, so scientists can only estimate, or guess, at their population. Scientists record the number of sea turtles on a beach and which nests are doing well. They compare these numbers from year to year. This tells them how well sea turtles are doing in general.

Track that Turtle!

Scientists are finding new ways to track sea turtles. Researchers put a tag on the turtle's shell. A microchip in the tag tracks the turtle by satellite wherever it goes.

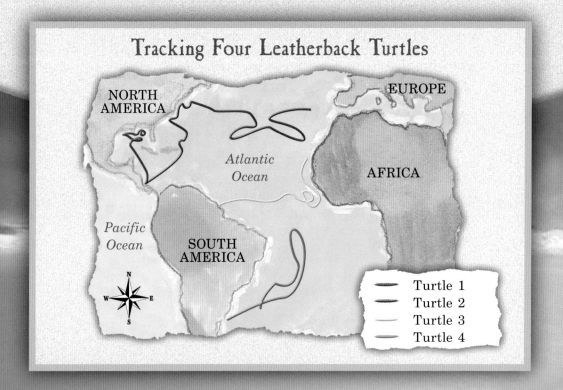

Tracking Four Leatherback Turtles

NORTH AMERICA — EUROPE — AFRICA — Atlantic Ocean — Pacific Ocean — SOUTH AMERICA

Turtle 1
Turtle 2
Turtle 3
Turtle 4

Where do you think this turtle might go?

Scientists also track sea turtles by putting the tags in the shoulder muscle of a nesting turtle. Sometimes they put numbered metal or plastic clips on a sea turtle's flipper. Some turtles have been tracked for years and years, giving researchers useful information about a turtle population's growth patterns and numbers.

Chapter Four

How Can You Help the Turtles?

There are six different kinds of sea turtles in U.S. waters: loggerhead, green, leatherback, hawksbill, Kemp's ridley, and olive ridley. All six are considered **endangered** and are protected by the U.S. government. This means that many people are working to keep these amazing animals safe.

However, sea turtles still need our help. That's why I'm thrilled to help these creatures in any way I can. My favorite part is helping the tiny hatchlings.

Maybe some day you could be a turtle person and help hatchlings find their way to the sea, too. If you are interested in becoming a turtle volunteer, learn as much as you can about sea turtles. Check out some sea turtle Web sites. Read books, watch educational shows on TV, and visit beaches with protection programs.

Sea Turtle Dangers

There is one simple thing you can do to help sea turtles. Be sure to recycle plastics, which sometimes end up in the ocean. Plastic bags are especially dangerous to sea turtles. The bags look like jellyfish, a favorite food of turtles. Once sea turtles realize their mistake, they can't spit out the bag. A turtle's mouth and throat are lined with spines to keep slippery jellyfish from escaping.

jellyfish

If a sea turtle eats a plastic bag by mistake, the bag can fill up the turtle's stomach and keep it from eating like it should. So remember, the next time you use a plastic bag, be sure to recycle it. And if you ever see a plastic bag on the beach, throw it away. You may save a sea turtle's life!

What kind of dangers might a sea turtle face in the open waters of the ocean?

Saving Sea Turtles

Today, I am the director of the Holden Beach Turtle Watch program. I continue to keep an eye on the beaches, search for nests, and help lost and hurt sea turtles. I visit local schools to teach children about helping sea turtles. With your help, we can turn the tide for these wonderful creatures.

I love working to help sea turtles. How can you help, too?

Let's Talk Turtle!

- Turtles are reptiles. There are about 270 species of turtles in the world.

- A turtle cannot crawl out of its shell. The shell is attached to some of the turtle's bones.

- Sea turtles have flippers instead of legs. They waddle through the sand rather than walking.

- The smallest turtle is the mud turtle, which grows to be about 3 inches long. The largest turtle is the 7-foot-long leatherback, which can weigh more than 1,000 pounds.

- Small turtles can live for up to 50 years. Large sea turtles may live for 100 or more years.

- Turtles do not have teeth. They use their sharp beaks to bite off plants or to crush insects and fish.

- A batch of eggs is called a clutch.

Glossary

banned not allowed, stopped

endangered in danger or at risk

extinct no longer living

hatchling baby turtle

natal beach a beach where sea turtles are born

pollution harmful materials that make the environment dirty

predator animal that hunts and kills other animals

relocate to move from one place to another

volunteer to do helpful work without pay

Index